DEAL

4 SIMPLE STEPS TO
RELEASE FEAR

KELLY JENNINGS

ISBN: 1975943872
ISBN-13: 9781975943875

ACKNOWLEDGMENTS

MUCH GRATITUDE TO EVERYONE WHO BELIEVED IN ME IN MY JOURNEY OF GETTING IT ALL DONE. TO MY FAMILY AND FRIENDS WHO ENCOURAGED ME TO STEP OUT IN WHAT YOU ALL BELIEVED I COULD DO. THERE WERE TIMES IT WAS ONLY YOUR FAITH THAT KEPT PUSHING ME TO THE FINISH LINE. I COULD NOT HAVE MADE IT WITHOUT YOU. THERE WERE MANY OBSTACLES, SETBACKS, FINANCIAL WOES, AND FRUSTRATIONS, BUT YOU NEVER LET ME GIVE UP.

,

KELLY JENNINGS

CONTENTS

Acknowledgments   iii

ABOUT THIS BOOK   vi

1   INTRODUCTION...............................   11

2   DEFINE THE FEAR...........................   15

3   EXAMINE YOUR EMOTIONS-------------   19

4   ANSWER THE CALL...........................   23

5   LET IT GO..   31

6   CONCLUSION   41

ABOUT THE AUTHOR...........................   43

ABOUT THIS BOOK

D.E.A.L is short for Define, Examine, Answer, and Let go. It is a series of teaching from my debut book "Quiet Storm." Quiet Storm is a small depiction of how I lived my life in pre- tense, behind pain, anger, hurts, and fears. It was not until I was willing to release the unknown person inside of me, get out of the boat and walk on water, was I able to D.E.A.L with the fear that was holding me ransom to my past. After years of watching many people fail at relationships, businesses, careers, and personal decisions, I discovered the common denominator was "FEAR."

My ability to teach on this

subject did not come without a battle in my mind myself. Having done many interviews for those who wish to change careers or start a new career, I realized that those who failed did not fail because of lack of ambition, knowledge, intellect or the ability to get it all done. They only failed because they were afraid. For years I struggled with fear, intimidation, and rejection. I concluded this was the main reason I could not complete my desired dreams.

I had all the knowledge, degrees, resources and more. However, I could not move beyond the mind paralysis because of fear. In my research, I found many quality leaders suffered from the same emotional deficit as me. Therefore, I followed my passion and decided to do something about this crippling emotion that affects so many people on a daily basis.

Unfortunately, most people don't realize they were not able to overcome their internal fears that kept them from moving forward. All too often I've seen many make significant financial investments and business risks before they counted the cost or realized that it took more than zeal to get it done, it took courage which is the opposite of fear.

D.E.A.L is designed for the faint hearted and for those who have the desire to do but lack the courage. Pushing past fear is the main ingredient to moving to your next level and living a successful life. We all have fear, some more than others. There are many great talented people still hidden in caves. While they hear the clarion call to come out of the caves, they are so afraid to take the first step. This book will help coach you and many others through the process of coming out of the cave, starting over and moving towards your destiny. You will do this while someone is holding your hand through the process of dealing with your fear. You can do it. I'm with you every step of the way.

QUOTES TO LIVE FOR:

1. A quiet mind is not always an idle mind.

2. Gain control of the mind...gain control of emotions.

3. Mental exercise is as important as physical exercise.

4. Fear doesn't kill you...it slows you down.

5. The way to overcome fear is to do it anyway!

6. Your destiny awaits you...so what are you waiting for?

7. If you transform your mind...your life must follow.

8. Pain is only a sign that something may be wrong...it's not a death sentence.

9. A willingness to deal with the hard places in life is a step towards healing.

1
INTRODUCTION

I believe the richest place in the world is the grave yard. Most people who die do so without fulfilling their life's destiny.
The grave is full of innovative and ground-breaking ideas such as cures for cancer, HIV, and many other chronic illnesses. Even some are unfulfilled multimillionaires and billionaires. Why did these people die taking such remarkable talent and solutions to the grave with them? I believe it is because they did not know how to M.I.N.D their business. I'm not suggesting these were people who died because of the trouble in their life. I'm suggesting that many died unfulfilled because they did not have the mindset to push past their fears and pursue the business they were sent to Earth to do.

What business do you say? Your business, your ministry, your book, your ultimate purpose in life, your health, your peace, your joy and so much more. Let's face it, everyone can have a physical business but most won't. So I'm not only writing to the entrepreneur or business owner. I'm writing to the home- maker, the stay-at-home dad, the CEO, the pastor, the author, the professional lawyer, the doctor, the accountant, the professor, and so many others.

Many of these people mentioned earlier are frustrated and unfulfilled. They know there is so much more inside of them, but they're stuck in the mind traps of life, disabled and paralyzed from past hurts, disappointments, failures, and portrayals. Many have dreams, passions, destinies and even suppressed pain trapped inside of them. The culprit to all of this is FEAR. That's why it's capitalized for a reason because fear is the reason most people remain stuck in the same dead job, relationship, ministry, and career for years.

Fear is a crippling emotion that attacks the mind. Realizing that the mind is the master computer that controls the function of the entire body, fear goes after the primary system of our lives. Why the mind? Because the brain can remember any and everything, we force our minds to do. Because of this highly capable skill, fear can train the mind to remember only the pain, the past hurts, the extreme trauma (even if it was years ago). Each time a person makes any effort to move forward in life, business, relationship, ministry or anything else, fear kindly reminds them of the pain they've suffered. So, many choose not to pursue life because the memory of the pain in the past is too much to get over. One thing is for sure if we want to win, we must D.E.A.L with the issues that are affecting our lives. Are You Ready?

Write your personal thoughts here.
What are you feeling right now?

_____

_____

_____

_____

_____

_____

_____

If you've gotten this far in the reading, you are likely one who said, "I'm tired of being bullied by fear. I am afraid, but I'm ready to do something about it." If this is you, like many others, your destiny awaits you, and you can no longer sit and wish fear away.

YOU MUST FIGHT...

I hope you are ignited and ready to do battle. Since you are still reading, I sense the fighter in you. You not only want to conquer fear...you want to be a CHAMPION in life. First, let me assure, you are not in this battle alone. I'm right here with you, and I won't leave you until you come out on the other side a champion. This guide will help advance your mind instantly and ignite the destiny call on your life. You will learn how to master fear and pursue your life destiny with confidence and courage. Today is the best day of your life. However, we must remember that life has a way of throwing a curve ball. We can't always control the life dealt us, but one thing is for sure if we want to win, we must D.E.A.L with some internal issues. Let's get started.

2
DEFINE THE FEAR

There is an old saying that states "what you don't know won't hurt you." I beg to differ. I believe at times, what you don't know can kill you. Therefore, to only say you have fear is not enough; you must explicitly define your fear. You must give fear a more definitive name. This does not mean you've taken ownership of fear in your life. I believe fear can be trans- formed to power, love and a sound mind. So we should not own fear as if it rightfully belongs, but We must identify the type of fear to tackle it the proper way.

Our biggest setback to fear is the power of denial. We all know we are to affirm ourselves in positive ways. Speaking positive, and removing all negativity in our lives. These are all good practices, and we should do them. But, what happens when we've done these things yet fear still remains? How do we explain the days when attacked with the thoughts of failure, success, or rejection? What words of affirmation do we use to help us get over this emotional deficit we struggle with on a daily basis?

Take Time to Define Fear:
Fear has many faces.
What are your fears? Be specific.

Fear of:
- Failure
- Love
- Success
- Trusting Others
- Rejection & Abandonment
- Past Hurts
- Believing
- Isolation
- Being Alone
- Poverty
- Etc.

Take time to list them:

Here's your diving board. Today, I admit that I'm afraid of: (list at least three of your strongest fears.)

1) _____
2) _____
3) _____

You Must Ask the Hard Questions

For the most part, we give fear too much authority in our lives. Fear roars like a lion, but too much of our surprise, it's bark is much bigger than it's bite. However, if we honestly combine the questions of what we're afraid of and why we're afraid; we may realize that fear is not as real as we make it.

However, those controlled by fear usually demonstrates a suspicious behavior, a lack of trust and a defensive attitude towards others. Additionally, they make up vain imaginations and establish false conversations in their mind to help them justify their fears. Running away from our troubles are one of our biggest defense mechanisms.

Some behaviors reflect in ways such as:

- Self-preserving (protective, a flight risk)
- Low self-esteem
- Self-sabotaging of relationships, business deals, and career elevations
- Nervousness
- Verbal or physical abuse
- Very defensive
- Easily offended
- These are just to name a few.

Can you identify with any of these behaviors? Hmm.

These are behaviors we must identify. Then, we must define the fear that aligns to the behaviors we are displaying. So let's do this again. What specific fear are you struggling with?

3
EXAMINE YOUR EMOTIONS

Throughout my life, I've discovered that many people revert to an extreme emotional state when fear is present. The correlation of fear and emotions is directly related. The strength of the fear in one's life is indicative in a person who is unable to control their emotion. I have found that individuals who are extremely emotional, are plagued with fear from past hurts.

These people normally have trust issues as well. Our emotions live in our soul. Here is where we make our decisions. We use our emotions to rationalize our behavior, hurts, and happiness. For the most part, we control our emotions well. However, there are times we become emotionally out of control, and we struggle with the ability to master our fears. Fear is an emotion authorized by God. A certain level of fear is there to protect us from harm and danger. It is this kind of fear that is there for a specific reason. It was never meant to torment us. Unfortunately, when we give fear access to our heart and mind, it takes us over. So, while we are supposed to control our fear, fear controls us. Then fear becomes a part of us and our conversation changes. Once we claim fear as a permanent entity in our lives, it becomes the things we talk about the most, and it's reflective in our actions.

Whoso keeps his mouth, and his tongue
keeps his soul from troubles.
Proverbs 21:23

Signs of a person bound by Fear:

Individuals who are full of fear may live with passive, aggressive behavior. At times, they let their emotions get the best of them. The fear that someone may get the upper hand over them sends them into a frenzy. Eventually, they calm down, but not until they've ruined the trust level in their relationships and has all of their close friends and loved ones on eggshells.

Normally, people who carry allot of fear are compulsive and make very irrational decisions. This is their defense mechanism kicking in which causes them to go into the immediate protective mode. When they do this, their walls are erected, and nothing or no-one can get through to them until they've had time to cool off and consider their actions.

Let's face it, all of us have some form of fear. Our body is conditioned to allow forms of fear to resonate in us. Particular fear protects us from danger or harming ourselves. However, the greatest indication that fear has gotten the best of a person is their inability to control their emotions in various situations.

I believe abnormal fear is a direct correlation of an excessive emotional person. Emotionalism is dangerous. If it remains uncontrolled, it likely leads to dangerous outcomes, outbursts of anger, rage, bitterness, and resentment. Fear is the culprit to most of these emotions. For example, when I feel overwhelmed I can typically trace it to some form of fear. Fear of success and failure will cause a person to retreat back to his or her comfort zone and remain trapped in procrastination and poor time management. This frequently leads to self-sabotaging behaviors. When a person becomes emotional, they will make decisions to leave a safe and healthy relationship, business, ministry or career. Sensitive people overreact and cause others to repel away from them. An individual who is full of fear allows their emotions to control them. Their life pattern is so familiar they've become accustomed to their behavior. They can't understand why they find it difficult to keep long term relationships or get along with others. In most cases, they have not critically examined themselves to become acutely aware of themselves. Therefore, I conclude that a person who can control their emotions is one who is full of wisdom and fearless.

4
ANSWER THE CALL

Where fear hovers, the most is a strong indication of the greatness fear is trying to suppress in you. Just think, if you have nothing to offer, why would fear try to keep you so bound. I have discovered those who carry so much fear lacks the clear understanding of their purpose and call on their life. Where there is great passion and clarity of purpose, fear has no power. A fully persuaded person with great passion gives little way to fear. Therefore, when you answer the call and the purpose you are called to fulfill fear can't keep you down long.

Consider these questions.

a. If you had nothing to offer in life, would fear exist?
b. Are you clear on what you've been called to do in life?
c. Are you afraid of the greatness in you?

Fear Fact:

The fact that fear exists is a good indication that you are on to pursuing or becoming something great in life.

Our deepest fear is not that we are inadequate. Our deepest fear is that we are powerful beyond measure. It is our light, not our darkness that most frightens us. You're playing small does not serve the world. There is nothing enlightened about shrinking so that other people won't feel insecure around you. We are all meant to shine as children do. It's not just in some of us; it is for everyone. And as we let our lights shine, we unconsciously permit other people to do the same. As we become liberated from our fear, our presence automatically liberates others.

Marianne Williamson Author, Lecturer

PASSION IS REAL

True Passion Weakens Fear
Answering the call does not mean fear will not be there. However, those who know and understand their purpose will not

let fear hinder them. Even though you may get discouraged and frustrated along the way, your passion will drive you past your fear. Passion is a deep love for something, and when you like something so strong, nothing can keep you from answering the call.

Okay, some of you may be saying, "I don't know what my call is." Well, your call could be the very thing that fears you.

"You don't start out looking like the person God called you to become." Kelly

We may not always have the knowledge or skill-sets to fulfill our life's purpose. However, our clarity of our purpose will cause our passion for driving us toward everything we need to be successful in life.

During times of helping people discover their purpose, after several sessions, we realized their call traced back the thing they feared the most. It may have been the past trauma they've been avoiding or the death of a loved one. You say, "How can these have anything to do with my purpose?" Many times, the very hurt, fear or problem is the thing we were born to pursue and solve.

I can't tell you how much joy it is helping people find their ultimate purpose in life. When the light finally goes off in their minds, it's so exciting. I've seen so many who denied their abilities one day and the next day they've taken their call by the reigns and they are achieving their life goals. It is so awesome when we understand our purpose and choose to

ANWER THE CALL.

You are greater and more qualified than you think you are. The fact that you have the burning desire to achieve something you've never done before speaks to your ability to get it done. The funniest thing about fear is that it can't hold a passionate person down for long. Passion drives out fear. It causes a person to push past fear to fulfill his or her life's call.

The drive and passion ooze out of them because their love for what they are called to do is so intense. In many cases, they achieve some of their greatest feats without ever recognizing fear, at least until it's all over.

If you're not sure of your purpose of call; pray and ask God to show you what you were born to do on this Earth. The caveat to this, is you must be willing to hear and accept what He may say. Besides praying, here are some simple steps you can take to help discover your call.

- Discover your strengths. There are several books out there that can assist you in this.
- Pay attention to your natural strengths.
- Observe the things that frustrate you most.
- Be willing to take a risk to pursue your purpose in life.
- Evaluate things you love to do and would do even if you never got paid.
- Ask your close friends what they see in you.
- Ask them to list some of your strengths and good qualities you possess

I don't recommend a constant seeking of everyone's opinion about you especially if your friends tend to be too critical, however, some of your close friend's perception of you can sometimes be healthy. Often it is difficult for us to notice our strengths because we tend to focus on our weaknesses more.

Your close friends are aware of your consistent strengths and weaknesses. So why not make yourself vulnerable among those you can trust? However, the process of moving from fear to freedom start with your willingness to be transparent to be read like an open book.

Releasing the Hidden You is about acknowledging you are in a Quiet Storm, and you are no-longer afraid to admit where you are mental, physically, spiritually, or emotionally. One of the hindrances about overcoming fear is the concern for the opinion of others and the need to be accepted by others.

These concerns may prevent you from becoming vulnerable and naked before others. If this is a major concern for you, then we may need to address a bigger issue than what's surfacing, and that is, are you as close to those you call your friends as you thought? Can you trust your confidence in their hands? Do you have a problem with being emotionally naked before those you call your friends? If you are unable to answer yes to any of these questions honestly, then you are living in a quiet storm. The bigger issue to consider

is why? Do your friends have the same problem with being open and transparent around you?

If they can, then the issue of transparency lies within you. What are you so afraid of, that you are unable to express to those you call your closest friends? Are you in an unhealthy relationship? Do you fear rejection? Do you fear isolation or abandonment? May you require some time to ponder?

I believe every man, woman, boy, and girl should have at least 1-3 people they can personally let down their hair around. It may take time to find these people, but we should not rest until we "Find Our Three." These people should be able to pour into your life and permitted to give you a good kick when you are getting out of line. I call them your accountability partners.

If you are uncomfortable with this requirement, then we must go back to square one and redefine your fear. There are likely some deep-rooted issues that you have not identified or willing to deal with at this time. Don't be discouraged, instead be thankful that you have just discovered another issue of your heart. The hidden thing is revealed, and you are now able to address some deep-rooted issues that may be the cause of some of your fears. Getting to the root-cause is a redundant process. You may have to go back several times to realign your priorities and discover which level of fear has the stronger hold in your mind, your emotions and in your heart.

5
LET IT GO

The only thing you are leaving behind is the thing that hurt you the most and the thing you feared. It's amazing how much power we give to our past. Unfortunately, our past is what keeps us from moving into the greater things in store for our lives. The crippling memory of the past can keep a person mentally paralyzed for a lifetime. Unable to fight the harsh realities of the last broken relationship or failed business can keep an individual stuck in the past. Releasing the pain and walking in healing and forgiveness is not easy.

You will likely discover that every step towards your purpose loosens the strength of fear. However, the greater your desire to seek your purpose the more fear will try to attack you. Fear is trying to prevent you from answering the call.

There are times you need additional help to let go

"When you're fearful...you justify fear's existence due to lack of courage."
~Kelly Jennings

Consider these questions?
a. What are the closed doors you're trying to pry open?
b. What is so important in your past, that you are unwilling to let it go?
c. How do you plan to use your past to propel you into your future?
d. Are your memories still as current to you as the day it happened?
e. Do you struggle with forgetting pain, whether physical or emotional?

"When one door closes, another opens; but we often look so long and so regretfully upon the closed door that we do not see the one which has opened for us."
– Alexander Graham Bell

Fear of the unknown, fear of failure, fear of success even fear of the future can keep a person constantly looking back. However, to properly DEAL with fear, one must decide to let go of the past so that fear can no longer hold onto you. I believe this step is the hardest thing to do. Essentially, when you make up your mind to let it go, you are relinquishing control of your past, and your emotions. For those who are believers, you've given God full permission to place you on the potter's wheel. Just as the potter begins to apply pressure to the clay to mold it in the image it desires, God does the same thing, Jeremiah 18: 1-6.

Because of the massive pressure to change and let go, many fail and do not endure the pressure. How- ever, those who will allow God to begin to pry their hands from the firm grip of their past. The individual will start to feel a release and to freedom to continue to distance oneself from his or her past hurts and fears. The joy of knowing that fear no longer has power over your life is liberating.

The Process of Releasing

When you decide to let go of past hurts, fears, disappointments, anxieties, etc., you've officially begun the process of releasing. You've chosen to get out of the boat and walk on water...no looking back, and please don't look down. Just keep your eyes on the prize. Remember, you are leaving the things you feared the most, the hurt, the pain, the negative words, the abuse, and the shame all behind you.

The choice to let go is solely yours; no-one can force you to do this. However, it's a pivotal point in your life if you are ready to deal with fear properly. Here are some simple steps to finally let go of fear.

- Choose to remember the pain no more.
- Ask yourself, what can this fear do to me?
- Earnestly forgive all those who hurt you in the past.

Many do not understand how walking in un-forgiveness can leave you crippled and stagnated in your emotions with the inability to move forward. However, when you choose not to forgive, it keeps you in the past, fearful of letting go of the pain, anger, resentment, hatred, etc. Ironically, the person you chose not to forgive has moved on with his or her life.

These steps though called simple and far from easy. It takes a made-up mind to let go of the past and move on. It's almost as if you have loyalty to the pain of your past. It's okay to let it go. It's okay to desire to be healed. It's good to say goodbye to your past.

When you choose to let go of your past, you will no longer have to contend with your past haunting you again. Letting go is easier said than done because this is where you will battle the most. II Corinthians 10:4 (Amplified), warns us that we must be ready to fight against every word or voice that attempts to bring us back in the bondage of fear.

The struggle with letting go likely stems from the fear of the unknown. You just don't know what lies ahead of you. I can assure you that your future is much brighter than your past. From this point on it's a step of faith. If after making this far in your reading and you still find it difficult to let go, then ask yourself these simple questions.

1. What is more important in my past that keeps me from being excited about my future?
2. When you try to step forward; what do you hear in your mind? Is it true?
3. Is the thing you're afraid of physical, emotional, mental, or spiritual?

Take time to ponder, be honest. Here's your diving board: When I think about letting go of my past fears I feel…

_____

_____

_____

_____

What measures do you feel you should take to get over the deep emotional fears?

- Professional counseling
- Contact Local Authorities; seek shelter
- Medical attention
- Life Strategy Skills/Mentor
- Healing and Deliverance

Take time to express what you are feeling right now. Are you excited about letting go? Are you still afraid? With either emotion, how do you feel?

When you make a radical move to DEAL with fear and let go of your past, you are awakening the sleeping giant within you. There are some who will say, "If it's not broke don't fix it." The truth is they don't realize there's a person inside of you waiting to explore the world and fear is keeping you from pursuing your life goals.

For years you were living in a quiet storm, and this is your time to re- lease the quiet storm in you. Others may say, "Don't disturb the sleeping giant." I say, "Wake him up and kick him out." You have no more room for monsters taking up space in your life and mind. The giant of fear in your life has lived in you for free too long. It's time to send an eviction notice and tell fear.

"FEAR...YOU MUST GO...
            Get your stuff and get out."

It's time to D.E.A.L with your fear and kick fear out of your life.

So, let's change our perspective about fear and see it in a different way:

Let's **F.E.A.R** it away:

   Face It,

   Examine It,

   Attack It, and

   Rule Over It.

Here are a few Bible readings to help you along the way.

II Corinthians 10:3-4 (amplified)

3-For though we walk (live) in the flesh we are not carrying on our warfare according to the flesh and using mere human weapons.

4. For the weapons of our warfare are not physical weapons (weapons of flesh and blood), but they are mighty before God for the overthrow and destructions of strongholds. Here are some empowering words to help you on your journey.

Jeremiah 18: 6 (amplified)

O house of Israel, can I not do with you as the potter does? Says the Lord, Behold, as the clay is in the potter's hand, so are you in my hand O house of Israel.

II   Timothy 1: 7 (amplified)

For God did not give us a spirit of timidity (of cowardice, of craven and cringing and fawning fear), but He has given us a spirit of power and love and of calm and well-balanced mind, discipline and self-control

6
CONCLUSION

Contending with fear is no laughing matter. Having dealt with anxiety myself, I can attest that breaking fear in your life is not easy. However, if you're ever going to become great in any aspect of life, you must D.E.A.L. with fear. Before you start another broken relationship or a failed business get the fear under control.

Fear is only as big as the image
you make in your mind.
~Kelly Jennings

When David stood up against the giant Goliath, he was not alarmed by how big Goliath was. He only knew that his God was greater. God's greatness was the only image David kept in his view.

Ask yourself these questions:

- Where is my faith?
- What image do I see when confronted with the giants in my life?

The key to overcoming and releasing fear is recognize that fear will always exist. However, it's your ability to **F.E.A.R** it away. Remember, fear did not come from God, but God never said, fear does not exist. You will find throughout the Bible where God tells His disciples to fear not and be of good courage. God understood that there would be times that we would fear. However, if we keep our focus on the one who gives us strength to go through the fear, we can declare the below scripture.

Psalm 23:4 "ye though I walk through the valley of the shadow of death; I will fear no evil" (KJV).

Move from fear to faith.

Work with Kelly:

If you are struggling with fear and you are tired of being held up by this crippling emotion, then you need to sign up for Kelly's mind-blowing transformation programs and move from fear to freedom. By taking the following steps, you will be on your way to total freedom. Here's what you should do next.

Visit my website at www.thekellyjennings.com or email at kelly@thekellyjennings.com

Sign up for a free 30-minute life strategy session http://workwithkelly@acuityscheduling.com

Visit my website at www.kellyjennings.net

Follow me on Facebook, Instagram, and Twitter @thekellyjennings. Like my Facebook page at Kelly Jennings–A

Prophet's Place. Take it a step further an join my closed group "Champion Culture" at bit.ly/champ777. Champion Culture is a place where champions unite. We have decreed that we will not quit, we will get it done.

Thank you for purchasing this book. Please be so kind to leave a review on my amazon page.   I would greatly appreciate it.

ABOUT THE AUTHOR

Kelly serves with her husband as the CO-laborer of Freedom to Live Ministries (FTL) in Fayetteville, GA. Kelly is a teacher to teachers, a speaker, a mentor, and a life strategist coach.

Her passion is to straighten the back of many women who are broken and bent over as well as restore families by empowering and encouraging men to take their rightful place back in the home. She is also a transformational leader who believes if "you transform your mind...your life will follow." She is the author of "Quiet Storm (ready for pre-order), "Delivered – 7 Days to Your Ultimate Freedom" and M.E.D.I.C.I.N.E for the Mind. She has several more such as "When Daddy is Not Enough" and "The Hidden Place" Kelly is a decorated retired the United States Air Force Master Sergeant. Her background skills of over 35 years culminating as Human Resource Management, Organizational Leadership, Program Management, Organizational Administration, and Pastoral Counseling. She received her Master's Degree in Business (MBA) from J. Mack Robinson School of Business, Georgia State University, Atlanta, Ga. and is currently pursuing her Doctorate in Christian Counseling.

Here's her testimony:

"For years, I struggled with fear. I was crippled in my mind, afraid of failure, rejection, and success. I realized that there was no way I could effectively help others If I could not break the fear that paralyzed me with the inability to move to the next level." I contended to become a champion in life. I realized fear would be there...I just had to fight through it. Together, let's DEAL with fear and move closer towards our destiny in life.'

Be not conformed in your thinking or to the business of the world: but be ye transformed by the renewing of your mind, that ye may prove what is good and acceptable, and the perfect will of God.

Romans 12:2 (paraphrased)

For more information about me visit www.kellyjennings.net and sign-up for my weekly inspirations. You can follow my teachings through Facebook, Periscope, and Instagram @thekellyjennings and Twitter at kellyajennings7

Upcoming Premier Books

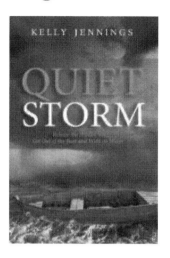

QUIET STORM:
Release the Hidden You

I didn't understand my anger, rage, hurt and fear that was suppressed within me. It was not until I was willing to face the pain of my past was I able to release the Quiet Storm, get out of the boat and walk on water. Discover how to release the quiet storm within you.

Available for pre-order now.

DELIVERED:

7 Days to Your Ultimate Freedom.

Delivered is a self-pace workbook manual. Each day, week or month you can address a different facet of fear and Discover how to overcome fear of rejection, failure, intimidation, procrastination and more. This workbook will assist you in identifying the root cause of your past hurts, pains, and disappointments, and empower you to live an amazingly productive life. After completing this book, you will receive new confidence and courage.

Available: 15 November 2017.

D.E.A.L

4 Simple Steps to Release Fear

Don't allow fear to hold you back another day. Discover the strategies to overcome fear. Develop the courage to release the quiet storm of fear hidden deep within you.   Available now through various distributions.

M.E.D.I.C.I.N.E FOR THE MIND:

Discover how to properly embrace the Necessities of Change by meditating on the daily regime needed to remain victorious in your mind. When we fuel the mind with the proper thoughts, behaviors, and "vitamins" of life, we are able to release the quiet storms in our lives in a more efficient way. Enjoy your daily affirmations for your mind and gain strength, confidence, and the courage to pursue purpose with passion.

Available 15 November 2017.

To hear more teaching from Kelly, follow Kelly on social media at: FaceBook, Instagram and Periscope @thekellyjennings Twitter @kellyajennings7

Join the

ChampionCulture Facebook Group
Where Champions Unite

At Bit.ly/champ777

We fight together, we win together, and may lose together, but regardless of the outcome, we always stay together.

To book Kelly for webinars, workshops or teaching/speaking engagements email us at kelly@thekellyjennings.com.

DEAL

Made in the USA
Columbia, SC
17 November 2017